English for Social Welfare

Communicative Skills for College Students

福祉の英語

William M. Balsamo・阿部敏之

KINSEIDO

Kinseido Publishing Co., Ltd.
3-21 Kanda Jimbo-cho, Chiyoda-ku,
Tokyo 101-0051, Japan

Copyright © 2002 by William M. Balsamo
　　　　　　　　　Toshiyuki Abe

All rights reserved. No part of this publication may be reproduced, stored in a retrieval system, or transmitted, in any form or by any means, electronic, mechanical, photocopying, recording or otherwise, without the prior permission of the publisher.

First published in 2002 by Kinseido Publishing Co., Ltd.

本文イラスト　佐藤衿子

はしがき

　今日の日本は，より成熟した共生の社会へと変貌しつつあります。民族や性別，年齢，障害の有無を超えて，人々が等しく心豊かな生活が送れる福祉社会に向かって進んでいます。国においても年金，医療，保険，保育といった問題にどのように適切に対応していくかということが21世紀初頭における大きな課題となっています。その意味で，これらの分野における情報や話題が急速に増えており，私たち一人ひとりにおいても，国内外のこれらの情報を正しく捉え，活用することが大切だといえるでしょう。

　本書は，最近の英字新聞や雑誌の記事を参考に，長年日本の大学で教鞭をとっている外国人教授によって書き下ろされた英文を軸として構成されています。日本人の福祉への意識や考え方，ＩＴやハイテク技術の活用，福祉の仕事に従事する人々の労働条件，諸外国の実状，NGOやボランティアのあり方など，幅広い話題を取り出し，大学や短大の学生にとって興味ある，しかも役立ちそうな内容について集めています。より読みやすく，理解しやすくなるように配慮し，この分野でよく使用される英語表現を含む日常会話や用語，さらにその話題について考える手助けになるような多様な設問を設けました。いわばオールラウンドなコミュニケーション能力が身につくように工夫しました。特に各ユニットの会話については，その話題にふさわしい臨場感あふれる効果音の入ったCDが付属しており，講義中はもちろんのこと各自が自由に練習できるように配慮されています。

　この本の作成にかかわって痛感したことは，これらの英文それぞれの底に流れるものは，相手の立場に立った人間としての温かい思いであり，ヒューマニズムの精神でありました。物質的豊かさのなかで心の貧しさが話題になる今日，これらの各ユニットの英文を通して英語力を養い，それぞれの課題について理解を深めるとともに人間としての自らの生き方を考える機会になれば幸いです。

平成13年10月10日　著　者

本書の使用法について

　本書は，福祉に関する15のトピックについての英文を軸に，次の5つのセクションを設けて有機的に構成されています。各課のタイトルの下にはその概略と課題を日本語で説明しており，スムーズに内容に入っていけるようになっています。各セクションのねらいは以下のとおりです。

WARM-UP DIALOG

　各課のトピックに基づいた会話文を付属CD（もしくはテープ）で聞くことで，基本的な会話表現を身に付けるとともに，その課の英文理解の導入的学習をします。会話文中には，いくつか空欄を設けてありますので，ダイアログの進展に合わせて言葉を推測し，聞き取り能力を身に付けて下さい。日本語訳も付けているので，参考にすることができます。

FOCUS ON KEY WORDS

　福祉や医療の分野でよく使われ，後の英文理解のキーとなる英語表現を設問形式で取り上げました。それらに習熟することで，以降のセクションに備えます。

GETTING READY TO READ

　短い英文を読み，それぞれの空欄に語群から選んで文を完成させます。各文はそれぞれ次の READING PASSAGE を理解するためのヒントになっています。

READING PASSAGE

　まとまった内容の英文を読み，その内容に関する設問A，Bの答えを考える中で，福祉についての理解を深め，それぞれのトピックについて考察します。
　設問Aでは，英文の内容に関する4～5つの設問があり，重要語句を選別することで英文の理解を確認します。
　設問Bでは，英文に関する質問を「英問英答」形式で答える練習をします。この設問で，英文の理解を深めて下さい。

WRITING PRACTICE

　本書で用いられている構文や表現を利用して，与えられた日本文に対応する英文を完成させ，英語での表現力を養います。

　以上のように，福祉についての幅広い情報を得ると共に，それについて考えることを通して，読み，聞き，話し，書く，の四つの領域での英語力を身に付けることを目指しています。どうか，楽しみながら学習してください。

CONTENTS

1. *Japan Still Behind in Accepting Physically Disabled People*　　6
　——日本人の福祉への理解は深まっているでしょうか？

2. *Crafts Help Disabled Win Independence*　　10
　——障害者にとっての働く意義とは？

3. *Providing Care and Laughs for the Elderly*　　14
　——老人の孤独をいやすのは何でしょうか？

4. *Medical Info Just a Phone Call Away*　　18
　——外国人が日本で病気になるとどんな苦労があるでしょうか？

5. *Program Allows Seniors to Utilize Videophones*　　22
　——ITは福祉の分野でどんな役割を果たすのでしょうか？

6. *Bedridden Elderly People Must Be Helped to Help Themselves*　　26
　——お年寄りが寝たきりになるのを防ぐにはどうしたらよいでしょうか？

7. *Discussion Is Necessary to Accept Nursing Care Workers from Overseas*　　30
　——介護の仕事を外国人にまかせられますか？

8. *Electronic Pets to Help Monitor the Health of City's Elderly*　　34
　——ロボットのペットが独居老人の命を守る

9. *Training Program Planned to Prepare Volunteer Drivers for Elderly*　　38
　——NPOは福祉の分野でどんな活躍をしているのでしょうか？

10. *Nursing Care Plan Creates Demand for Home Helpers*　　42
　——介護保険制度導入に伴うホームヘルパーの労働条件

11. *Service Dogs Strive for Official Recognition amid Ignorance*　　46
　——障害者を支える犬は盲導犬だけでしょうか？

12. *Baby-Sitter Exam Aims to Improve Care*　　50
　——安心して子どもをベビーシッターにまかせるためには？

13. *Japan Braces for Life as Oldest Nation*　　54
　——世界一の長寿国日本，高齢者の世話は誰がするのでしょうか？

14. *Ex-Nissan Chief Says Nation Is Ill-Prepared for an Aging Society*　　58
　——どうして日本は，高齢化社会への対応に遅れてしまったのでしょうか？

15. *Simulated Patient Enables Risk-Free Medical Training*　　62
　——マネキンが医療や介護教育の手助けになるでしょうか？

1 JAPAN STILL BEHIND IN ACCEPTING PHYSICALLY DISABLED PEOPLE

日本人の福祉への理解は深まっているでしょうか？

障害を持つ人々に対する考え方はさまざまに変わってきています。私たちは，障害者に対してどの程度理解を深めているでしょうか。障害者とともに住みよい社会を築くために，私たちは何をすべきでしょうか？

WARM-UP DIALOG

CD TRACKS 1–2

▶日本語を参考に，CD を聴いて（　　）に適切な語を入れましょう。

Mariko: Excuse me, can I (1　　　　) you?
Satoru: Yes, please. I want to cross the street but there is much traffic.
Mariko: O.K. Please take my hand and I will help you to go across.
Satoru: Thank you. I sometimes get (2　　　　) crossing busy streets.
Mariko: Just hold my hand. There is no reason to be nervous. I'll walk (3　　　　) your side.
Satoru: I worry that a car might hit me by (4　　　　).
Mariko: Don't worry. People are here to help you.

*　*　*　*　*

Satoru: You are very kind to see me across the street.
Mariko: It's my (5　　　　).
Satoru: Thank you for your help.

真理子：お手伝いしましょうか？
悟：はい，お願いします。通りを渡りたいのですけれど，交通量が多いものですから。
真理子：わかりました。私の手につかまってください。ごいっしょしましょう。
悟：ありがとうございます。通りを渡る時には不安になるものですから。
真理子：私の手を握っていてくれれば，ご心配には及びません。あなたのそばを歩きますから。
悟：あやまって車に轢かれるのではないかと思って。
真理子：大丈夫。みんながお手伝いしますよ。

*　*　*　*　*

悟：助けていただいて本当にすみません。
真理子：どういたしまして。
悟：ありがとうございました。

FOCUS ON KEY WORDS

▶次の１から５の単語の意味を，a～eより選んで，線で結びましょう。

1. street crossing　　・　　・a. 手話
2. wheelchair　　　　・　　・b. 横断歩道
3. blind people　　　 ・　　・c. 視覚障害者
4. sign language　　　・　　・d. 点字
5. Braille　　　　　　・　　・e. 車椅子

GETTING READY TO READ

▶次の（　　）に，下の語群から適語を選んで入れてみましょう。

1. In the past life for the disabled was very (　　　　) but today social awareness of the needs of the handicapped has made it easier.
   昔は，障害を持つ人たちの生活は厳しかったが，今日では障害者が必要としていることへの社会の理解が進み，より楽になりました。

2. If we help the handicapped the world will become a (　　　　) place for everyone.
   私たちが障害者を支援するならば，すべての人にとってより住みよい社会になります。

3. Yellow tiles (　　　　) raised surfaces are used on train platforms to guide the blind.
   駅のホームで用いられている表面がでこぼこの黄色いタイルの道を歩くと，目の不自由な人も安心して歩けます。

4. It has become more (　　　　) to find Braille both in restaurants and stores.
   最近では，レストランでも商店でも点字が使われているのが見かけられるようになりました。

common / difficult / better / worse / with / have / best / in

READING PASSAGE

▶英文を読んで，設問A，Bに答えましょう。

　There are about three million disabled people in Japan. The life of handicapped people in Japan is better today than before. For example, for blind people there is music at street crossings to help them. Also, special buses have lifts and ramps for wheelchairs. In addition there are public toilets for handicapped people in most places.

　However, both the government and most people do not fully understand the special needs of the handicapped. Countries in northern Europe, for example, have advanced facilities for the disabled. In Japan people still do not realize that helping the handicapped will make the world a better place for everyone to live.

　During World War II people made fun of handicapped persons in Japan. They were called "worthless" because their disability prevented them from fighting for their country. When the war ended in 1945 a large number of disabled soldiers came back from the front line and the government found it necessary to help them. Also at that time many disabled people demanded their rights. Since then laws helping the handicapped have been passed.

　In addition, their living conditions have become easier. Yellow tiles, for example, with raised surfaces can often be found on sidewalks and train stations throughout the country to help the blind. Such tiles were introduced in the sixties. They are used a lot on train platforms so that people who step on them know that they should not walk any further.

　Although still not very common, some restaurants have introduced Braille menus and some department store clerks can use sign language. But, these measures are far from enough. What we need now is to make the public aware of the problems faced by the handicapped everyday.

Notes : not fully …「十分に～ではない」　make fun of …「～をからかう」　prevent A from B「AがBできない」　front line「戦線」　living conditions「生活状態」　throughout the country「国中で」　not … any further「これ以上～しない」　clerk「店員」　far from …「～からほど遠い」

A 本文に合うように，文中の（　　）の中から適語を選びましょう。

1. The music at street crossings helps (the aged persons / blind people / children) to cross the streets.

2. One of the countries which has advanced facilities for the handicapped is (India / Denmark / Brazil).

3. (All people / Not all people / No people) fully understand the special needs of the handicapped.

4. Disabled people began to demand their rights (during / after / before) World War Ⅱ.

5. Yellow tiles can often be found (in the middle of the streets / on the sidewalks / on the railroads).

B 本文の内容を踏まえて，下の質問に答えましょう。

1. In what way is the life of handicapped people in Japan better today than it was before?

    Because there is (　　　　　) at the street crossings for (　　　　　) (　　　　　) and special buses for wheelchairs.

2. How many disabled people are there in Japan?

    There are about (　　　　) (　　　　) disabled people in Japan.

3. In what year did World War Ⅱ end?

    It ended in (　　　　　).

WRITING PRACTICE

▶READINGの英文を参考にして，次の日本語を英語に直しましょう。

1. 北欧の国々では障害者に対する施設は進んでいます。

2. 最近では，デパートの店員さんの中にも手話ができる人が増えてきました。

3. 今日の日本で大切なことは,障害者が何を必要としているかを誰もが知ることです。

2 CRAFTS HELP DISABLED WIN INDEPENDENCE

障害者にとっての働く意義とは？

これは，一人の女性が障害者のために開いた工房で，老若男女が種々の労作に携わりながら，人生に充実感と喜びを感じる取り組みの紹介です。働きながら共同生活をすることの大切さについて考えましょう。

WARM-UP DIALOG

CD TRACKS 3–4

▶日本語を参考に，CD を聴いて（　　　）に適切な語を入れましょう。

Michiko: Oh, these ceramics are very beautiful!
Staff Worker: Yes, they show the work of great talent.
Michiko: And these skirts have wonderful patterns and (1　　　)!
Staff Worker: Yes, they were also (2　　　) by one of our members.
Michiko: It must (3　　　) them a long time to do such fine work.
Staff Worker: Oh, it does! But they enjoy it.
Michiko: Their talent is very professional.
Staff Worker: Yes, and they are (4　　　) to have the chance to express themselves through their work.
Michiko: I think I would (5　　　) to buy one of these ceramics.
Staff Worker: A good choice! And the profit goes directly to the artist who made it.

美知子：まあ，この瀬戸物本当に美しいわ。
職員：ええ。ご覧の通り，相当な腕前ですよ。
美知子：また，このスカートは模様といいデザインといい，すばらしいですね。
職員：ええ，これもここのメンバーの作品です。
美知子：こんな細かい仕事だとずい分時間がかかることでしょうね。
職員：その通り。でもみんな楽しんでいますから。
美知子：皆さんの腕ってプロ並みですね。
職員：そうですよ。でもみんな作品を通して自己表現するいい機会と考え幸せに思っていますよ。
美知子：わたし，この瀬戸物をひとついただくわ。
職員：お目が高いですね。この利益は作品を作った人のところにいくのですよ。

FOCUS ON KEY WORDS

▶次の1から5の単語の意味を，a～eより選んで，線で結びましょう。

1. cerebral palsy　　　　　　　　　　・　　　　・ a. 自給自足できる
2. people with mental disabilities　・　　　　・ b. 障害者用施設
3. sense of achievement　　　　　　・　　　　・ c. 達成感
4. self-sufficient　　　　　　　　　　・　　　　・ d. 脳性麻痺
5. facility for the handicapped　　　・　　　　・ e. 知的障害者

GETTING READY TO READ

▶次の（　　）に，下の語群から適語を選んで入れてみましょう。

1. A small shop in Setagaya, Tokyo employs handicapped people both (　　　　　) and old.
   東京，世田谷の小さな店は，老若を問わず障害者を雇っています。

2. The workshop hopes to become a place (　　　　　) the handicapped can learn new skills.
   その作業所は，障害者が新たな技術を身につける場所になることが望まれています。

3. Ms. Takenouchi established a workshop (　　　　　) the disabled in Portland, Oregon.
   竹内さんは，オレゴン州のポートランドに障害者が働く作業所をつくりました。

4. The trips to the United States have become very (　　　　　) and give the handicapped an international experience.
   アメリカへ出かけることが大変人気となり，またそれが障害者にとってよい外国での生活体験になりました。

   where / popular / fashion / for / young / small / in / which

READING PASSAGE

▶英文を読んで，設問Ⓐ，Ⓑに答えましょう。

　It is difficult for people with handicaps to find work. Some companies are afraid that they cannot do a good job, so they will not hire them. In 1983, however, Mutsuko Takenouchi, a Tokyo mother with three children decided to set up a dyeing shop called Ai-kobo with a friend who suffers from cerebral palsy. Ai-kobo means "indigo workshop." This small shop has a small staff with some volunteers but also hires people with mental and physical handicaps.

　The shop is located in a large building in Setagaya, Tokyo. The members are both young and old from teenagers to people in their eighties. Nevertheless, the sound of laughter fills their workshop. They work on a variety of projects. Some dye materials, others make ceramics and embroidery. The items made in the workshop go on sale. The price tag for each item includes the name of the person who made it. This gives the maker a sense of pride in his work.

　Ms. Takenouchi did not want the workshop to become just a factory but rather a place for the disabled to develop skills. It was a chance for them to become productive and independent.

　In addition to the workshop there is also a café and gallery. They were opened in 1996 for people with mental disabilities. This café, however, is the same as other cafés in Japan and most customers can not tell the difference.

　In 1998 Ms. Takenouchi opened a place for the handicapped in the U.S. near Portland, Oregon. She believed the disabled could experience daily life more easily in the U.S. than in Tokyo. Already about 600 people have stayed at the facility. The length of the stay is up to the individual. Some stay for a month, while others may stay longer. However, volunteers are needed at the facility and many of them find it a challenging experience. The trips to the U.S. have become very popular and Ms. Takenouchi is eager to find more volunteers who can speak English and help her with her work. She is indeed a good example of someone who cared enough to make a change even though she is the busy mother of three children.

Notes: be afraid that …「～を怖れている」　suffer from …「～で苦しむ」　embroidery「刺しゅう」　set up「設立する」　go on sale「売りに出す」　dye「染める」　productive「創造的な」　indigo「藍色の染料」　in their eighties「80歳代の」

A 本文に合うように，文中の（　　）の中から適語を選びましょう。

1. The handicapped people who worked in the workshop felt (happy and satisfied / sad and unhappy / happy but unsatisfied).

2. The items made in the workshop were (presented to them / given to them / put on sale).

3. On the price tag, there was also the name of (the workshop / the person who set up the workshop / the person who made the item).

4. The café is no different from an ordinary one, so customers (do not notice / find soon / see easily) that it is run by the handicapped.

B 本文の内容を踏まえて，下の質問に答えましょう。

1. When did Ms. Takenouchi decide to set up a dyeing shop?
   She decided to set up the shop in (　　　　).

2. What kind of work do the handicapped people do in Ai-kobo?
   Some (　　　　) (　　　　), while others (　　　　) (　　　　) and (　　　　).

3. Why does the price tag for each item include the name of its maker?
   Because this gives the (　　　　) a (　　　　) (　　　　) (　　　　) in his work.

WRITING PRACTICE

▶READINGの英文を参考にして，次の日本語を英語に直しましょう。

1. 彼は，自分の仕事を手伝ってくれるボランティアを探し求めています。

2. 日本ではまだ障害のある人が自分の好きな職業を見つけることは難しい。

3. 障害者のための作業所はこの建物の2階にあります。

3 PROVIDING CARE AND LAUGHS FOR THE ELDERLY

老人の孤独をいやすのは何でしょうか？

人間は他人との温かいふれあいがあって初めて孤独から開放されます。これは，病院でケアされていた父親を家庭につれて帰り，家族とともに暮らすことにした娘と孫娘の善意の話です。その努力は報いられるでしょうか？

WARM-UP DIALOG

CD TRACKS 5-6

▶日本語を参考に，CDを聴いて（　　）に適切な語を入れましょう。

Mariko: Old people need friends just like everyone else, don't they?
Kumiko: Yes, that's true. In fact, maybe they need friends (1　　　) than younger people.
Mariko: I think so too.
Kumiko: As one gets older it's easier to (2　　　) sick and lonely.
Mariko: Especially when close friends and family die.
Kumiko: That's (3　　　) a day-care center can make old people feel happy.
Mariko: It becomes a place where they can feel useful and laugh with people (4　　　) their own age.
Kumiko: When they laugh with friends, they don't feel lonely (5　　　).
Mariko: And helping others makes them feel useful.
Kumiko: I think you're right.

真理子：老人だって若い人と同じで，友達が必要じゃないのかなあ。
久美子：その通りよ，むしろ若い人たちより余計に必要とするのじゃない？
真理子：私もそう思う。
久美子：人間って年齢を重ねるにつれて気が沈み勝ちになって孤独になるのよ。
真理子：特に親しい友達や家族が亡くなるとね。
久美子：デイケアセンターがお年寄りを明るくさせるのもそのためでしょう。
真理子：そこは，自分が人のためになる人間だと思える場所であり，年の違わない人たちと笑顔を交わせる場所となるのよね。
久美子：仲間と一緒に笑顔で居られるともはや孤独感に陥ることはないよね。
真理子：それに，他人に尽くせば存在感ももてるしね。
久美子：そう思うわ。

FOCUS ON KEY WORDS

▶次の１から５の単語の意味を，a～eより選んで，線で結びましょう。

1. a day-care center   ・   ・ a. 高齢化が進む町
2. aging town   ・   ・ b. 孤独に悩む
3. to suffer from loneliness   ・   ・ c. 高齢者
4. welfare association   ・   ・ d. 社会福祉協議会
5. the elderly   ・   ・ e. デイケアセンター

GETTING READY TO READ

▶次の（　　）に，下の語群から適語を選んで入れてみましょう。

1. At a daycare center for senior citizens in Miyagi the sound of singing and (　　　　) greets the visitor.
   宮城県の高齢者デイケアセンターでは，歌と笑い声が訪問者を迎えます。

2. Ms. Sasaki hopes to set a model for her children by taking (　　　　) of her father.
   佐々木さんは，父親のケアをすることで子供たちにお手本を示そうとしています。

3. Because the (　　　　) of elderly people increased each week, Ms. Sasaki had to find a bigger place.
   １週間ごとに高齢者が増えるので，佐々木さんはもっと大きな部屋を探さねばなりませんでした。

4. Elderly people have taught her a (　　　　) and now she knows what to expect when she gets old.
   彼女はお年寄りの人たちから学ぶことが多く，今では自分が年を取った時にどうすべきかが分かるようになりました。

   care / part / laughter / crying / lot / much / number / size

READING PASSAGE

▶英文を読んで、設問A, Bに答えましょう。

Visitors who come to a daycare center for the elderly in Miyagi Prefecture will be surprised to find it filled with singing and laughter. Mariko Sasaki is the head of the center called "Mari's House in Exciting Wakuya." Wakuya-cho is a small town of 20,000 people where 20 percent of the population is over 65 years old.

She got the idea for a daycare center for senior citizens when she was taking care of her weakening father. Mariko is one of many Japanese who face the problem of taking care of an aged or sick family member.

She used to be a food vendor but now heads a group of caregivers in charge of about 30 elderly people. Her life was changed by her daughter when they visited her father in the hospital. Her daughter suggested they should take her father home with them.

After much thought she decided to take care of her father at home. She thought this would be the best example to set for her own children. She felt that by keeping her father in the hospital she was running away from the responsibility of taking care of him.

Her father came to live with Mariko and her family in 1995 but he became quieter day by day and began to become unhappy. At first, Mariko did not know what made him so sad and then realized that he needed friends.

In 1996 she started a weekly daycare project at her home. At first, five elderly people came to be with her father. Every week the number increased until she realized that she needed a larger place. The town's mayor saw the situation and allowed her to use a public building.

The new day-care center opened in January 1998 and the town's welfare association hired four staff members to help her. At the center the elderly passed the time singing, making origami and preparing lunch. But, they especially come to chat and laugh. Through her work Sasaki believes that many old people are not happy at home. Many suffer from loneliness even when they live with their children. She is proud of what she and her staff are doing. She also feels that she has learned a lot from the elderly. They have taught her what to expect when she gets old and she is better prepared for her silver years.

Notes: prefecture「県」 used to be ...「昔は〜であった」 population「人口」 be in charge of ...「〜に責任を負う」 run away from ...「〜から逃げる、回避する」 come to live with ...「〜と一緒に住むようになる」 day by day「日一日と」 sign「兆し」 increase「増加する」 pass the time ...ing「〜して時間を過ごす」 one's silver years 「〜の老年期」

A 本文に合うように、文中の（　　）の中から適語を選びましょう。

1. The population in Wakuya-cho is as (many / large / great) as twenty thousand.

2. (What / That / Which) her daughter suggested to Mariko when they visited their father in hospital changed Mariko's life.

3. Mariko thought (much / little / a little) before she decided to take care of her father at home.

4 The reason why the mayor allowed Ms. Sasaki to use a public building was that (more and more / less and less / the same number of) aged people wanted to be with her father at her home.

B 本文の内容を踏まえて、下の質問に答えましょう。

1. How many old people over sixty-five do you think live in Wakuya-cho in Miyagi?

    About (　　　　) (　　　　) people live in Wakuya-cho.

2. What was Mariko's job before she became the head of the center?

    She was a (　　　　) (　　　　).

3. Why was her father unhappy even after he was taken home from the hospital?

    Because he had (　　　　) (　　　　).

WRITING PRACTICE

▶READINGの英文を参考にして、次の日本語を英語に直しましょう。

1. 日本では家族で高齢者の世話をするという問題に直面する家庭が多い。

2. 家で家族が介護しても、お年寄りは孤独になることがわかりました。

3. その福祉施設には、6名の職員がいてお年寄りとおしゃべりしたり食事の用意をしています。

4 MEDICAL INFO JUST A PHONE CALL AWAY

外国人が日本で病気になるとどんな苦労があるでしょうか？

国際化が進み，日本で生活する外国人が増えています。言葉が十分でないこの人たちが病気になったり，身体が不自由になった時，どんなことで困っているのでしょうか。その対応は十分でしょうか。

WARM-UP DIALOG

CD TRACKS 7–8

▶日本語を参考に，CDを聴いて（　　）に適切な語を入れましょう。

Doctor: May I help you?
Patient: Yes. I am not feeling (1　　　　).
Doctor: Well what is your problem?
Patient: It's difficult to explain because I can't (2　　　　) Japanese well.
Doctor: Well, what is your native (3　　　　)?
Patient: I am (4　　　　) Australia. I speak English.
Doctor: That's no problem. We have doctors here who can speak English very well.
Patient: Oh, that's great to hear!
Doctor: Yes, in fact Dr. Tanaka studied in Sydney for four years.
Patient: Sydney? That's my (5　　　　).

医者：どうされました？
患者：ちょっと体調が思わしくなくて。
医者：どこがお悪いのですか？
患者：うまく説明できないのです。日本語がうまくないのです。
医者：お国はどちらですか？
患者：オーストラリアです。英語を話します。
医者：じゃあ，問題ありません。うちには英語をしゃべれる医者がおりますから。
患者：それはありがたいです。
医者：実は，田中医師は4年間シドニーに留学していました。
患者：シドニーですって。わたしの故郷です。

FOCUS ON KEY WORDS

▶次の１から５の単語の意味を，ａ〜ｅより選んで，線で結びましょう。

1. treatment　　　　　　　　　・　　　・ a. 兆候
2. information on hospitals　・　　　・ b. 病院に関する情報
3. medical records　　　　　　・　　　・ c. 緊急医療施設
4. emergency facility　　　　・　　　・ d. 診療記録
5. symptom　　　　　　　　　　・　　　・ e. 手当，処置

GETTING READY TO READ

▶次の（　　　）に，下の語群から適語を選んで入れてみましょう。

1. Osaka has an information center which gives the names of hospitals (　　　　) sign language is used.
   大阪には，手話が使われる病院の名前を教えてくれるインフォメイション・センターがあります。

2. Many foreigners living in Japan often face language problems (　　　　) they want information about hospitals.
   日本に住む多くの外国人は，病院についての情報が欲しい時にしばしば言葉の問題に直面します。

3. Doctors in Japan used to keep medical records in German (　　　　) now many find that English is more useful.
   昔は日本のお医者さんは，カルテをドイツ語で記録していましたが，今日では，英語の方が便利であると考える人が多い。

4. Now many hospitals in Japan have questionnaires in English (　　　　) that patients can answer questions about their illness more easily.
   今日では，日本の多くの病院で，外国人の患者が自分の病状についてより簡単に答えられるように英語で質問項目が書かれています。

which / when / where / how / so / and / but / who

READING PASSAGE

▶英文を読んで，設問Ⓐ，Ⓑに答えましょう。

　Foreign residents sometimes have difficulties in finding information about hospitals which give treatment in their own language. This causes many problems and can make a difference in the treatment they receive. Osaka is one of the few cities with an hourly service offering information on hospitals with doctors who can speak a foreign language. Unfortunately, the service is available only in Japanese.

　In Osaka there is an information center which answers questions as to the number of empty beds in a local hospital and a list of places with emergency facilities. They even have information about hospitals where sign language is used.

　The number of calls tends to be greater between 6 p.m. and midnight and jumps again early in the morning. Because the service is available only in Japanese, few foreigners call for information. Furthermore, the center's phone is listed only in the Japanese media so it is not easy for foreigners to use.

　However, other prefectures have also followed the example to give medical information for foreigners in Japan. Foreign residents of Japan's major cities get easy access to volunteer organizations when they become sick, but this is not always true for those who live in the countryside where there are less facilities.

　In the past doctors kept medical records in German, but today many of them have recently begun to use English. Although many doctors can usually read the English used in medical records, many are still hesitant if a patient speaks a foreign language. To solve this problem many prefectures now publish a guidebook which offers advice on everyday problems and includes emergency telephone numbers. Some also have local volunteers who speak foreign languages and will go with foreigners to a doctor to serve as an interpreter.

　Also many prefectures have a bilingual questionnaire where patients can write details of their symptoms and give details of their family's medical history. These are typical ways by which medical aid can be made easier for foreign residents.

Notes: make a difference in …「〜に差が出る」　hourly「1時間ごとの」　be available「〜が利用できる」　tend to「〜する傾向にある」　call for「要求する，求める」　not always「いつも〜であるわけではない」　countryside「地方，田舎」　hesitant「ためらっている」　bilingual「2か国語の」　typical「典型的な」

A 本文に合うように，文中の（　　）の中から適語を選びましょう。

1. The number of phone calls from foreigners tends to be less (in the daytime, / at midnight, / in the early morning) at the center.

2. Until recently medical records had been written in (Japanese / English, / German).

3. Some prefectures have local volunteers who speak English and other foreign languages and serve as (doctors, / nurses, / interpreters) in the hospital.

4. Many prefectures nowadays have questionnaires where patients can answer (in English only, / in Japanese only, / either in Japanese or in English).

B 本文の内容を踏まえて，下の質問に答えましょう。

1. What difficulties do foreign residents face in Japan when they become sick?
   They face difficulties in (　　　　)(　　　　)(　　　　) hospitals.

2. What information does the Information Center of Osaka give?
   It gives the number of (　　　　)(　　　　), a list of places with (　　　　)(　　　　) and information about hospitals where (　　　　)(　　　　) is used.

3. What is meant by "bilingual questionnaire"?
   A "bilingual questionnaire" is a series of questions written in (　　　　)(　　　　).

WRITING PRACTICE

▶READINGの英文を参考にして，次の日本語を英語に直しましょう。

1. 日本に住む外国人は，病気になった時に病院についての情報を得るのに苦労します。

2. そのセンターに問い合わせると，緊急医療施設についての情報が得られます。

3. その医療施設では，家族の病歴などについて細かく聞かれます。

5. PROGRAM ALLOWS SENIORS TO UTILIZE VIDEOPHONES

ITは福祉の分野でどんな役割を果たすのでしょうか？

相手の姿を見ながら話ができるビデオ電話の出現が高齢者の孤独を癒したり，自室にいながら買い物を可能にするなど，障害者や高齢者に大いに役立っています。ここではITと，福祉の仕事との関連を考えましょう。

WARM-UP DIALOG

CD TRACKS 9-10

▶日本語を参考に，CDを聴いて（　　）に適切な語を入れましょう。

Yumi: Hello, Tomoko, how are you?
Tomoko: I am (¹　　　). You are looking very well today?
Yumi: Oh, can you see me?
Tomoko: Yes, of (²　　　) I can see you from my videophone.
Yumi: I can see you too! I see you have a new (³　　　).
Tomoko: Yes, I had it done yesterday. Do you like it?
Yumi: Yes. It is very nice. I feel that you are (⁴　　　) here with me and not so far away.
Tomoko: Yes. I know what you mean. It's just like being (⁵　　　) TV.
Yumi: Oh, before I forget, let me show you a picture of my new granddaughter.
Tomoko: I can see her very well on the video screen. She is beautiful.

由美：やあ，友子さん。元気？
友子：ええ，元気よ。今日は調子よさそうね。
由美：わかる？
友子：もちろんよ。このビデオ電話でよく分かるわ。
由美：わたしもよ。ところでヘアスタイル変えたのね。
友子：ええ，昨日ね。気に入ってくれる？
由美：すてきよ。この電話で話すとあなたがここにわたしと一緒にいるって感じ。とても遠くに離れているとは思えない。
友子：その通りね。テレビに映ってるみたい。
由美：そうそう，忘れないうちに言っておくけど，新しく生まれた孫の写真お見せするわ。
友子：まあ！ビデオ電話でもはっきり見えるわ。可愛いわね。

FOCUS ON KEY WORDS

▶次の１から５の単語の意味を，a～eより選んで，線で結びましょう。

1. senior citizen　　　　・　　　・ a. 人間生活の質
2. to enjoy chatting　　 ・　　　・ b. 孤独を癒す
3. confined to the home ・　　　・ c. おしゃべりを楽しむ
4. to ease the loneliness ・　　　・ d. 高齢者
5. quality of human life ・　　　・ e. 家に閉じこもる

GETTING READY TO READ

▶次の（　　）に，下の語群から適語を選んで入れてみましょう。

1. Senior citizens can now use videophones which (　　　　) them to see the person they are speaking to.
   高齢者の人たちも今日では，相手を見ながら通話ができるビデオ電話を使うことができます。

2. Some elderly people thought that the videophone was (　　　　) difficult to use.
   お年寄りの中には，操作が難しくてビデオ電話が使えないと考える人もいます。

3. At first some of the elderly were nervous about using the phones but later enjoyed (　　　　) them to talk with their friends and family.
   最初は，電話をかけるのに不安がる老人もいましたが，やがて友達や家族と話をするために使うことを楽しむようになりました。

4. Videophones are very (　　　　) for elderly people who are confined to their beds and who still want to see their friends.
   ビデオ電話は，寝たきりであっても仲間に会いたいと思う高齢者に大いに役立ちます。

---

enable / unable / too / enough / using / to use / useful / useless

READING PASSAGE

▶英文を読んで，設問Ⓐ，Ⓑに答えましょう。

A program has been tested to allow senior citizens to enjoy face-to-face phone conversations from the comfort of their own homes. Such videophones are very popular with older people.

With this new technology, senior citizens can maintain an active social life by exchanging New Year's greetings. The videophones help to ease the loneliness of many elderly people who cannot leave their homes.

The new videophones have been tested first in the Tokyo area but may soon be used throughout the country. The program received a mixed reaction from the elderly. Some people liked it very much saying that the system had saved them the trouble of going outside. Others complained that these phones were too difficult to use.

However, once the elderly were able to master the simple push of buttons the use of the videophones became easier than expected. Some of the phones were connected to food shops and the users were able to examine fish and vegetables and to place an order for food by means of the phone. Most of the elderly liked the idea of viewing products through the videophone screens.

At first many of the participants were nervous about the videophones but they gradually became more relaxed and enjoyed chatting over the phones with their family and friends. Gradually, their conversations became more lively and they discussed health and other problems.

When interviewed about the use of these phones their reaction was generally positive. Some said, "We feel closer to each other because we can see each other on the screen."

When this system becomes popular it will help senior citizens to become more involved with their communities, even though they may have to stay in bed. With the videophones they may be able to see loved ones living in another city and old friends who are confined to the home. It is another case of how simple technology can improve the quality of human life.

Notes： face-to-face「面と向かって」　than expected「思った以上に」　place an order「注文する」　by means of「を手段に使って」　participant「参加者」monitor「監視する，聴取する」　be involved「～にとけこむ」

A 本文に合うように，文中の（　　）の中から適語を選びましょう。

1. The videophones help many elderly people feel (more / less / very) lonely at home.

2. The new videophones tested first in the Tokyo area will eventually be used (only in Tokyo / in and around Tokyo / all over Japan).

3. To use the videophones, the elderly (need much trouble / have only / have no simple way) to push the buttons.

4. This passage tells us how (useful / useless / difficult) this simple technology is to improve the quality of human life.

B 本文の内容を踏まえて，下の質問に答えましょう。

1. What do the videophones allow senior citizens to do?

   The videophones allow senior citizens to enjoy (　　　　)-(　　　　)-(　　　　) phone conversations.

2. What are the reactions of aged persons who joined the first test of videophones in Tokyo?

   Some people (　　　　) (　　　　) very much, and others complained they were (　　　　) (　　　　) to use.

3. What did the elderly persons say at the interview about the use of videophones?

   Some said, "We feel (　　　　) to (　　　　) (　　　　)."

WRITING PRACTICE

▶READINGの英文を参考にして，次の日本語を英語に直しましょう。

1. このビデオ電話のおかげで，老人たちは相手の顔を見ながら話ができます。

2. このビデオ電話は食品店に接続されており，消費者は画面上で品物を見て，注文することができます。

3. Eメールで情報の交換が楽しめるようになると，お年寄りたちを孤独から解放することが出来ます。

6 BEDRIDDEN ELDERLY PEOPLE MUST BE HELPED TO HELP THEMSELVES

お年寄りが寝たきりになるのを防ぐにはどうしたらよいでしょうか？

お年寄りが体調を崩すとすぐ床を敷いて休ませてあげることが寝たきりへの道に繋がることにならないでしょうか？今，国や各都道府県で高齢者自立の取り組みがなされています。どんなことが課題なのでしょうか。

WARM-UP DIALOG　　　　　　　　　　　CD TRACKS 11–12

▶日本語を参考に，CD を聴いて（　　　）に適切な語を入れましょう。

Mariko: How does your mom feel today, Yoshiko?
Yoshiko: Oh, she is much (1　　　) than she was last week.
Mariko: Is she bedridden or can she (2　　　) about?
Yoshiko: Well, she is now back on her feet and more independent.
Mariko: Oh, what do you (3　　　)?
Yoshiko: Well, she's becoming more positive in her thinking about being old.
Mariko: So is she changing her (4　　　) of thinking?
Yoshiko: In a way, yes. She does not always (5　　　) upon me to do everything for her.
Mariko: Well, that's good news.
Yoshiko: Yes. I think by helping herself more she has become healthier.

真理子：佳子さん。今日はお母さんいかが？
佳子：先週に比べるとずっとよさそうよ。
真理子：寝たきり，それとも動けるの？
佳子：そうね，もう歩けるようになり，自分で動けるようになったの。
真理子：それ，どういう意味？
佳子：彼女，年取っているってことについての考え方により肯定的になってきたの。
真理子：考え方が変わりつつあるってこと？
佳子：ある意味でその通り。今までのようにすべてのことについて私に頼りっきりでなくなったのよ。
真理子：そう。それはいいことね。
佳子：そうなのよ。自分のことは自分で出来ることが健康でいることにつながると思うの。

FOCUS ON KEY WORDS

▶次の１から５の単語の意味を，a～eより選んで，線で結びましょう。

1. music therapy　　　　　・　　　　・ a. 在宅ケアサービス
2. home-visit care services　・　　　　・ b. 寝たきり状態になる
3. health problem　　　　・　　　　・ c. 健康問題
4. stroke　　　　　　　　・　　　　・ d. 音楽療法
5. to become bedridden　　・　　　　・ e. 卒中

GETTING READY TO READ

▶次の（　　）に，下の語群から適語を選んで入れてみましょう。

1. In some cities housewives visit the (　　　　) at home to give them advice or to help them feel better through music.
   家庭の主婦が高齢者の家を訪ねて助言したり，音楽で快適になるように援助している市もあります。

2. In order to reduce the number of strokes among the elderly some cities make sure that at (　　　　) one room in their home is kept warm.
   高齢者の脳卒中を減らすために，その家の少なくとも一部屋は暖房しているのかを，確認している市もあります。

3. By increasing the number of visits to homes and (　　　　) facilities health officials hope to improve the lifestyles of the elderly.
   保健所員が家庭や介護施設を訪問する回数を増やすことによって，高齢者のライフスタイルの向上に努めています。

4. The nursing care services need to be improved in order to prevent the elderly (　　　　) becoming bedridden.
   高齢者が寝たきりにならないようにするために，介護サービスは向上されなければなりません。

   from / by / elderly / young / last / least / nursing / taking

READING PASSAGE

▶英文を読んで，設問A，Bに答えましょう。

　Recently there has been a strong belief that one must look after one's own health. In many prefectures throughout Japan there are various programs designed to teach older people how to help themselves. For example, in some places the city has asked some local housewives to visit elderly people in their homes to offer advice about health problems. In addition, some places offer music therapy sessions. The elderly get better by singing songs.

　In cases where elderly people cannot go to a dentist, home visits are also provided. Since there are some people who can no longer chew, it becomes difficult for them to eat. As a result they become weak and are more likely to become bedridden.

　Campaigns in some cities have gone so far as to make sure that at least one room in every elderly person's home is kept warm. The purpose is to help reduce the cases of strokes which occur more frequently in colder regions. If the elderly have healthier lifestyles, the number of the bedridden will be reduced by 50 percent in the future.

　The Japanese government intends to work out a new ten-year plan to increase health programs for the elderly. It was put into effect in the fiscal year 2000. The plan allows those in need to be examined by doctors from time to time with the intention of helping them to lead healthier lifestyles. As a result, there will be an increase in the number of home visits and nursing homes.

　Also, more research is needed on such illnesses as Alzheimer's disease which affects the elderly. Many sufferers of such an illness may require 24-hour nursing care. This will be an impossible burden for families who take care of the elderly by themselves. Therefore, it is important to have better nursing care services to prevent the elderly from becoming bedridden. Japan needs to be a leading nation of the 21st century as her society grows increasingly gray.

Notes： look after「世話をする，介護する」　help oneself「自立する」　in case「～の場合は」　therapy session「治療機会」　be likely to「～しそうである」　no longer「もはや～でない」　work out「やり遂げる」　put into effect「実行する」　from time to time「折にふれ，時折り」　as a result「その結果」　research「研究，調査」　require「要求する」

A 本文に合うように，文中の（　　）の中から適語を選びましょう。

1. Hopefully the number of the bedridden elderly will be reduced by (10 / 25 / 50) percent in the future.

2. A new 10-year plan by the Japanese government was started in (January / April / September), 2000.

3. In the Japanese government's plan, the elderly will regularly be given physical examinations by doctors, and the number of home visits and nursing homes will (decrease / increase / not change).

4. A person suffering from Alzheimer's disease may well need (twenty-four / twelve / two) hours' nursing care.

B 本文の内容を踏まえて，下の質問に答えましょう。

1. What is a recent strong belief about elderly people?

   The recent strong belief is that they must look (　　　　) (　　　　) (　　　　) (　　　　).

2. What will become of the elderly when they can no longer chew nor eat?

   In such cases they are more likely to (　　　　) (　　　　).

3. What is the purpose of the campaigns in some cities to make sure at least one room in every elderly's home is kept warm?

   The purpose is to reduce (　　　　) (　　　　) of (　　　　).

WRITING PRACTICE

▶ READINGの英文を参考にして，次の日本語を英語に直しましょう。

1. 最近では，多くの県でお年寄りが寝たきりにならないようにするための施策が講じられるようになりました。

2. 老人が健康を害して歯医者に行けないようなときには，訪問治療がなされます。

3. アルツハイマーのような病気は昼夜の介護が必要であり，介護する人にとって大きな負担となります。

7. DISCUSSION IS NECESSARY TO ACCEPT NURSING CARE WORKERS FROM OVERSEAS

介護の仕事を外国人にまかせられますか？

少子化と高齢化が進むわが国ではやがて労働人口が減少し，介護の仕事を外国人に頼らなければならないことが考えられます。そのような場合にそなえて，解決しなければならない課題について考えてみましょう。

WARM-UP DIALOG

CD TRACKS 13–14

▶日本語を参考に，CD を聴いて（　　　）に適切な語を入れましょう。

Taro: I hear that someday foreign workers will come to Japan to (1　　　) for the elderly.

Kumiko: That's because our society is (2　　　) too quickly.

Taro: But do you think it will create problems?

Kumiko: How do you mean?

Taro: Well, don't you think there will be problems with (3　　　) and cultures?

Kumiko: Not really. When foreigners live in Japan they come to learn about Japanese society.

Taro: I guess you're right.

Kumiko: I am sure they will be (4　　　) and helpful.

Taro: I think so too. After all, in many ways people all (5　　　) the world are the same.

Kumiko: Yes, we need to think more globally.

太郎：将来は外国人が日本へ来て高齢者の介護をする時代が来ると聞いているよ。

久美子：日本は急速に高齢化が進んでいるからよ。

太郎：しかし，問題が起こると思わない？

久美子：それ，どういう意味？

太郎：言葉や文化の違いが問題になると思わないかね。

久美子：そうは思わないわ。外国人も日本に住み着けば，日本について理解できるようになるよ。

太郎：そうだろうね。

久美子：外国人は親切で大いに助かるわよ。

太郎：僕もそう思う。結局いろいろな面で世界中の人々は同じだということだよね。

久美子：そうよ。わたしたちはもっとグローバルにものを捉えなければならないよね。

FOCUS ON KEY WORDS

▶次の１から５の単語の意味を，ａ～ｅより選んで，線で結びましょう。

1. the graying of society ・   ・ a. 出生率低下
2. labor shortage ・   ・ b. 労働条件
3. working conditions ・   ・ c. 社会の高齢化
4. nursing care programs ・   ・ d. 介護計画
5. the declining birthrate ・   ・ e. 労働者不足

GETTING READY TO READ

▶次の（　　　）に，下の語群から適語を選んで入れてみましょう。

1. In the future many (　　　　　) workers may be employed in nursing care facilities in Japan
   将来は，日本の介護施設で多くの外国人が雇用されるかも知れません。

2. Some people believe that the Japanese government should not (　　　　　) too much on foreign workers in the nursing care field.
   日本政府は，介護の分野で外国人に頼り過ぎるべきではないと考える人もいます。

3. Many Japanese do not want to work in the nursing care field because they are not satisfied with the working (　　　　　).
   日本人の中には，労働条件に満足できないために介護の仕事につきたくないとする人が多くいます。

4. When foreign workers come to Japan they bring their own (　　　　　) with them and may not understand Japanese society.
   外国人が日本で働くようになると，彼ら自身の文化を持ち込み，日本の社会が理解できないことも考えられます。

depend / take / cultures / history / overseas / Japanese / conditions / salary

READING PASSAGE

▶英文を読んで，設問Ａ，Ｂに答えましょう。

There is now concern over a plan to allow overseas workers to take on nursing jobs in Japan. Most nursing care jobs are regarded as unskilled. The Foreign Ministry nevertheless wants to accept foreigners in nursing care because there may be a labor shortage due to the graying society and declining birthrate.

While Japan's working population will start to decrease after 2005, the number of elderly people needing nursing care will double in 2025. During this time more workers will be needed in nursing care services.

To revive the Japanese economy a group recently visited some Southeast Asian countries and proposed that foreigners be allowed to work in nursing care programs to help the nation's economy.

Yet this may be a problem. Foreign workers come to Japan and bring with them their own cultures and social backgrounds. They may not completely understand Japanese culture and society. It is necessary, therefore, for such workers to be on genuinely friendly terms with the elderly, just as though they were from the same family.

However, many believe that the government should not be too hasty to depend upon foreign labor in the nursing care field. They propose we should encourage quality workers in Japan to enter the field by giving them better opportunities. By creating good working conditions and good salaries the system could attract the best people available. Some believe that foreign workers in the nursing field would cause salaries to fall. This would cause Japanese workers to lose interest in such jobs.

More than half a million people have already completed training to become home helpers but the number of those who are actually working in the field is only about 170,000. The figure is disappointing. Many do not want this work because they are dissatisfied with the working conditions. Although nursing care work is physically demanding some workers are paid less than 1,000 yen an hour, the same as part-time workers. It is necessary, therefore, to make nursing care a respected profession in order to support social welfare in Japan for both foreign workers and Japanese.

Notes: be regarded「とみなされる」 be hasty to ...「急いで~する」 depend on ...「~に依存する」 lose interest「利益を失う」 be dissatisfied with ...「~に不満である」 encourage「励ます」 be on friendly terms with ...「~と親しくいく」 disappointing「がっかりさせる」

A 本文に合うように, 文中の（　　）の中から適語を選びましょう。

1. The number of the working population in Japan will begin to decrease after (2025 / 2005 / 2000).

2. The number of elderly people in 2025 who will need nursing care will be (as many as / twice as many as / three times as many as) now.

3. More and more Japanese people would go into the field of nursing care, if the (the working conditions / the working place / the government's plan) were improved.

4. Of those who have finished the training to be a home helper, nearly (one-third / half / all) have actually taken work in the field.

B 本文の内容を踏まえて, 下の質問に答えましょう。

1. What does the Japanese Foreign Ministry want to do to solve the problem of labor shortage in the field of nursing-care?

   The Foreign Ministry wants (　　　　) (　　　　) (　　　　).

2. What are two reasons why the working population in Japan will begin to decrease early in the 21 century?

   The reasons are the (　　　　) (　　　　) and (　　　　) (　　　　).

3. Give one reason against inviting foreign workers in the nursing-care field?

   One reason is that foreign workers would cause (　　　　) (　　　　) (　　　　).

WRITING PRACTICE

▶READINGの英文を参考にして, 次の日本語を英語に直しましょう。

1. 我が国ではやがて労働者不足のため介護の分野でも外国人を採用する時代がくるでしょう。

2. 労働条件が改善されれば福祉の分野で働きたいと思う若者は増えるでしょう。

8. ELECTRONIC PETS TO HELP MONITOR THE HEALTH OF CITY'S ELDERLY

ロボットのペットが独居老人の命を守る

コンピュータでモニターできる装置を内蔵したペットが独居の老人に声をかけ，老人の反応が行政機関でモニターされ，異常があると判断されると救急車が駆けつけて対応する事例です。ハイテクと福祉の関連を考えましょう。

WARM-UP DIALOG

CD TRACKS 15–16

▶日本語を参考に，CD を聴いて（　　）に適切な語を入れましょう。

Sumiyo: My grandfather got a new pet.
Ryugo: Really? What (¹　　　) of a pet is it?
Sumiyo: You'll never guess.
Ryugo: Is it a dog? A cat?
Sumiyo: It's (²　　　). It's a robot!
Ryugo: You must be (³　　　). I've heard of Aibo but they are not for old people.
Sumiyo: But this one is different. It's especially designed to help older people and to make them feel (⁴　　　) lonely.
Ryugo: Is it shaped like a dog?
Sumiyo: Oh, no. It is in the form of a wombat. Very cute.
Ryugo: Maybe I should get one for (⁵　　　).

須美代：うちのおじいちゃん，新しいペットを飼うことになったのよ。
隆吾：ほんと？種類は何？
須美代：見当つかないでしょう。
隆吾：犬？それとも猫？
須美代：どっちも違う。実はロボットなの。
隆吾：冗談でしょう。アイボの話は聞くけどあれはお年寄り向きではないしね。
須美代：お年寄りの手伝いをしたり，淋しさを癒すように作られた特殊なペットよ。
隆吾：犬の格好しているの？
須美代：いいえ。ウォンバット（フクログマ）の姿でとても可愛いのよ。
隆吾：僕も一つ欲しくなったよ。

FOCUS ON KEY WORDS

▶次の 1 から 5 の単語の意味を，a～e より選んで，線で結びましょう。

1. municipal government　・　　　・ a. 救急車
2. response　　　　　　　・　　　・ b. 保健所員
3. ambulance　　　　　　・　　　・ c. 緊急時に
4. health officials　　　　・　　　・ d. 反応
5. in case of emergency　・　　　・ e. 市役所

GETTING READY TO READ

▶次の (　　) に，下の語群から適語を選んで入れてみましょう。

1. Electronic stuffed animals will soon be used to help check on the health of (　　　　) citizens.
   そのうちに，電子装置が内蔵された動物が，お年寄りの健康チェックを手伝うために利用されるでしょう。

2. The electronic pets can offer simple greetings to their owners who can (　　　　) if they need help.
   電子ペットは飼い主に簡単なあいさつができ，飼い主は必要ならそれに応答します。

3. If there is an emergency, officials from the city (　　　　) can speak directly to the person through a small speaker placed inside the pet.
   緊急事態が起これば，市役所の職員がペットに内蔵されている小さなスピーカーを通して，すぐに飼い主のお年寄りに話しかけることができます。

4. The electronic pets (　　　　) wombats, gentle furry animals which are not likely to frighten older people.
   電子ペットはウォンバットの姿をしたやさしい毛皮で覆われた動物で，お年寄りを怖がらせたりしそうにもありません。

resemble / look / senior / junior / government / building / respond / want

READING PASSAGE

▶英文を読んで，設問Ⓐ，Ⓑに答えましょう。

　　The Ikeda municipal government in Osaka prefecture has used stuffed toy animals with a built-in computer to check on the health of elderly people. These electronic pets will soon be introduced into the market on an experimental basis.

5　　This is a new attempt to computerize the field of care for the elderly. If it proves to be effective, it will be used by many other prefectures throughout the country.

　　These electronic pets can say simple sentences and phrases such as, "Good Morning," and "It's a nice day, isn't it?" If the owner is not feeling
10　well he can respond to the pet and someone can come to help him.

　　In order to monitor these robotic pets city health officials will be linked with the homes of the "pet" owners by a cable TV. An antenna attached to the pet will relay conversations it has with its owner to the health officials. They will then use the information to decide if help is needed.

15　　In cases of special emergencies, a miniature speaker installed in the pet enables the officials to speak directly with the elderly. If there is no response, an ambulance will soon be sent to the home of the elderly person. These pets are now being tested and will be distributed on request when the trial period ends in 2004.

20　　The pets resemble wombats which are quiet, docile animals and not likely to frighten the elderly. It is estimated that about 1,000 elderly people live alone in Ikeda, a city of about 100,000. The number is expected to rise in the near future. The municipal government of Ikeda has already provided 165 sick and elderly people with a device that
25　notifies health authorities in case of emergency.

　　The city also employs other workers to help elderly residents with everyday household jobs. However, these home helpers are not under any obligation to inform authorities about the physical condition of the people they help. The virtual pets will assist in keeping better tabs on
30　the elderly.

Notes：built-in「組み込まれた」　on an experimental basis「実験を踏んで」　computerize「コンピュータ化する」　field of care「介護の業界」　robotic pet「ロボットのペット」

attached to ...「~に取り付けられている」 by way of 「を使って」 on request 「希望に応じて」 docile 「おとなしい，従順な」 authorities 「当局，権力」 be capable of ...「~ができる」

A 本文に合うように，文中の（　　　）の中から適語を選びましょう。

1. By way of (a microphone / a television set / a miniature speaker) installed in a pet officials can speak directly with the elderly.

2. In Ikeda city, in (2000 / 2004 / 2005) the electronic pets will be available to any elderly person who wants one.

3. The number of elderly people in Ikeda who live alone is (10 / 1 / 0.1) percent of the population.

4. In Ikeda city, (20 / 165 / 100,000) sick and elderly residents have used devices that can notify health authorities in case of emergency.

B 本文の内容を踏まえて，下の質問に答えましょう。

1. What device does the Ikeda municipal government use to check on the health of elderly people?

    The Ikeda municipal government has used (　　　) (　　　) (　　　) with a (　　　)-(　　　) (　　　).

2. What are two simple sentences and phrases which the electronic pets can say?

    They can say, "_____" and "_____."

3. What are two reasons why the electronic pets are in the form of wombats?

    Because wombats are (　　　), (　　　) animals and not likely to (　　　) (　　　) (　　　).

WRITING PRACTICE

▶READINGの英文を参考にして，次の日本語を英語に直しましょう。

1. その新しい携帯電話は，実験期間が終わればすぐに市場に出回るでしょう。

2. 緊急の場合には，電話をすればすぐに救急車が患者の家に派遣されるでしょう。

3. 市の方ではさらに80名のホームヘルパーを採用する予定です。

9. TRAINING PROGRAM PLANNED TO PREPARE VOLUNTEER DRIVERS FOR ELDERLY

ＮＰＯは福祉の分野でどんな活躍をしているのでしょうか？

高齢者や障害者が病院や買い物に出かけたいと思っても，ままならない苦労があります。そこであるNPO（非営利団体）がタクシー代わりをつとめる取り組みをはじめましたが，ここにも多くの課題があります。考えてみましょう。

WARM-UP DIALOG

CD TRACKS 17–18

▶日本語を参考に，CDを聴いて（　　　）に適切な語を入れましょう。

Fumiko: Is it true that you work now as a volunteer to help the elderly?
Toshiaki: Yes, I've been working as a volunteer now (1　　　) six months.
Fumiko: Oh, what exactly do you do?
Toshiaki: Well, sometimes I drive the elderly to an amusement park or a day (2　　　) into the countryside.
Fumiko: I think it's wonderful that you give (3　　　) your time to help the handicapped.
Toshiaki: But, really I (4　　　) doing it and I also have a good time.
Fumiko: Would I also be able to help as a volunteer?
Toshiaki: Sure, we are always looking (5　　　) more people to help us in our work.
Fumiko: But I think I can only give up one afternoon a week.
Toshiaki: One afternoon is fine. Say, why don't you come to our volunteers' meeting tomorrow?

文子：あなた，最近お年寄りのお手伝いをするボランティアしてるってほんと？
敏明：そうだよ。もう６ヶ月になるけどね。
文子：あらそう。どんなことをしているの？
敏明：そうだね，時にはお年寄りと遊園地や地方へ日帰り旅行に出かけたりしているよ。
文子：自分の時間を障害者の人たちのために使うなんて素晴らしいことじゃない？
敏明：だって，自分も気に入っているし第一楽しいよ。
文子：私もボランティアとしてお手伝いできるの？
敏明：できるとも。僕たちの仕事を手伝ってくれる人を探しているんだよ。
文子：１週間に１度，午後だけしか時間はとれないのよ。
敏明：それだってありがたいよ。あすの僕たちのミーティングに参加しようよ。

FOCUS ON KEY WORDS

▶次の1から5の単語の意味を，a～eより選んで，線で結びましょう。

1. non-profit organization ・   ・a. ボランティアの善意に頼る
2. to depend on the good-will ・   ・b. 福祉センター
   of volunteers   ・c. 安全基準
3. retired person   ・   ・d. 退職者
4. safety standard   ・   ・e. 非営利団体
5. welfare center   ・

GETTING READY TO READ

▶次の（　）に，下の語群から適語を選んで入れてみましょう。

1. Sometimes (　　　) persons or housewives may volunteer to help service the elderly by driving them in their own cars.
   退職した人や主婦が，よく自分の車で高齢者の人たちを送り迎えする仕事を手伝うのにボランティアとして参加します。

2. There are almost five hundred volunteer (　　　) in Tokyo which transport disabled persons to hospitals and recreational areas.
   障害者を病院や娯楽場所へ案内するボランティア団体が，東京だけでも約500ほどあります。

3. It is important to establish a good driver's training program to assure the (　　　) of the services which help the handicapped.
   障害者を運ぶ仕事の安全を確保するためには，優良運転者訓練制度を確立することが大切です。

4. Those who drive the elderly from one place to (　　　) should also know how to help them get in and out of vehicles.
   高齢者を車で運ぶ人たちは，高齢者の人たちが安全に車に乗り降りするのを手伝うこともできなければなりません。

   some / another / retired / retiring / organizations / people / safety / pleasure

READING PASSAGE

▶英文を読んで，設問A，Bに答えましょう。

　Driving services now help disabled and elderly people to be part of the community. Being run by volunteers and non-profit organizations, they are becoming very popular. These non-profit organizations depend on the good-will and driving ability of volunteers. These drivers are often older, retired persons or housewives and businessmen who give up a free day to service the elderly and handicapped by using their own cars.

　To get younger drivers, these organizations have established their own driver training programs to guarantee the safety of their service and to expand their activities.

　There are now close to five hundred volunteer organizations in Tokyo alone which transport the disabled and elderly people to hospitals, welfare centers and parks. They may even take them to shopping malls where they can spend an afternoon searching for bargains.

　Because the vehicles used are driven by volunteers these non-profit organizations generally charge low fees to cover the cost of operation. Most organizations, however, do not have taxi service licenses and volunteers usually only have regular driving licenses. There is, therefore, a great need to establish a driver's training program to guarantee public trust in the services they offer. Not only do these non-profit organizations want to trust in the driving experience of volunteers, they also want to set up safety standards.

　At a special conference in Tokyo in November of 1999 the need to train volunteer drivers was a main topic for discussion. At the conference guidelines for training methods were discussed. Under the proposal it was decided that trainees would learn how to effectively communicate with the elderly and the handicapped. Furthermore, special classes would teach safe driving techniques and how to help the elderly get in and out of cars.

Notes：be run「運営される」　good-will「善意，好意」　techniques「技能」　vehicles「乗物，器」　charge「料金をとる」　low fee「安い料金」　guarantee「保証する」　public trust「社会の信頼」　set up ...「～を創設する」　close to ...「～に接近している」　trainees「訓練生，訓練を受ける人」

A 本文に合うように，文中の（　　）の中から適語を選びましょう。

1. Driving services by non-profit organizations to help the elderly people are becoming popular (in Tokyo alone / throughout Japan / widely in Tokyo).

2. A non-profit organization is one whose members work for their communities or their nation and receive (no money / salary / wages).

3. There are (nearly / over / less than) five hundred volunteer organizations in Tokyo.

4. As the driving services are offered by non-profit organizations, the elderly people (need not pay any money / pay only a little money / need to pay much money) for the services they receive.

B 本文の内容を踏まえて，下の質問に答えましょう。

1. Who make up the volunteers offering driving services for the elderly and handicapped?

   They are (　　　　) persons, (　　　　　) and (　　　　　).

2. At a special conference in Tokyo in 1999, what was talked about?

   At the conference they talked about the need (　　　　) (　　　　　) (　　　) (　　　　).

3. Give the reason why these organizations have established their own driver training programs.

   They need to establish the programs because they want to (　　　　　) (　　　　) (　　　　).

WRITING PRACTICE

▶READINGの英文を参考にして，次の日本語を英語に直しましょう。

1. 非営利団体による障害者の社会参加促進運動は，全国に広がった。

2. ボランティアによる運転サービスによって，障害者が安心してスーパーへ行き，買い物が楽しめるようになった。

3. この提案に基づいて，介護者が高齢者と効果的な意思疎通ができるようになった。

10 NURSING CARE PLAN CREATES DEMAND FOR HOME HELPERS

介護保険制度導入に伴うホームヘルパーの労働条件

公的介護保険制度の導入に伴い，ホームヘルパーの需要は急速に増大しています。このような状況のもとで，ホームヘルパーをはじめとする福祉の仕事に携わる人々の労働条件に問題はないのでしょうか？

WARM-UP DIALOG

CD TRACKS 19–20

▶日本語を参考に，CDを聴いて（　　　）に適切な語を入れましょう。

Sachiko: Mariko, what do you plan to do after (1　　　　)?
Mariko: I've been (2　　　　) of becoming a home helper.
Sachiko: A home helper? Is that something like a (3　　　　)?
Mariko: Not really. You don't have to study as long but it is still an important job.
Sachiko: What exactly do you (4　　　　) to do?
Mariko: We are trained to help people who cannot leave their homes.
Sachiko: You mean, like some kind of babysitter?
Mariko: Well not exactly. It is much (5　　　　) challenging and requires special training.
Sachiko: Is it difficult?
Mariko: It requires a great responsibility, but I think it is rewarding.

佐知子：真理子さん，あなた卒業後どうするつもり？
真理子：ホームヘルパーになろうと考えているの。
佐知子：ホームヘルパーに？それって，看護婦さんに似た仕事？
真理子：あまり似てはいないのよ。看護婦になるためのように沢山勉強しなければならないことはないけど，働き甲斐のある仕事よ。
佐知子：一体どんなことをしなければならないの。
真理子：訓練を受けて家から出られない人たちの介助をするの。
佐知子：ベビーシッターに似たような仕事なの？
真理子：正確に言えば違うわ。この仕事の方がずっと魅力的だし，訓練が必要なの。
佐知子：その仕事は難しいの？
真理子：責任重大なの。でも報いも大きいと思うわ。

FOCUS ON KEY WORDS

▶次の1から5の単語の意味を，a～eより選んで，線で結びましょう。

1. income　　　　　　　　　　・　　　　　・a. 生計を立てていく
2. social welfare professionals ・　　　　・b. 収入
3. part-time worker　　　　　・　　　　　・c. 社会福祉専門家
4. to make a living　　　　　・　　　　　・d. パート労働者
5. new wage system　　　　　・　　　　　・e. 新賃金制度

GETTING READY TO READ

▶次の（　　）に，下の語群から適語を選んで入れてみましょう。

1. Job openings for home helpers have been rapidly increasing over the past years as the (　　　　) for their services is in greater demand.
   ホームヘルパーの仕事に対する需要が増大するにつれて，この数年間その求人は増え続けています。

2. Most home helpers are part-time workers who receive poor (　　　　) for their services and little job security.
   ホームヘルパーの仕事に対する給料が低く，安定性に欠けることから大部分の人はパートの仕事として働いています。

3. In order to support their families many home helpers have to supplement their (　　　　) by working a second job.
   ホームヘルパーの多くは，自分の家族の生計を維持するために別の仕事をしながら家計の不足分を補っています。

4. To improve working (　　　　) the Ministry of Welfare and Labor will give financial assistance to companies that provide nursing care services.
   労働条件を改善するために，厚生労働省は介護サービスを提供する会社に財政的補助金を出すことにしています。

conditions / hours / income / cost / pay / rent / need / supply

READING PASSAGE

▶英文を読んで，設問A，Bに答えましょう。

In April 2000, a new nursing care insurance system for the elderly started and job openings for home helpers are rapidly increasing. Over the past year the number of openings for home helpers has increased by threefold in Tokyo alone.

In the past there were a mere 12 job openings nationwide for social welfare professionals for every 100 applicants, but that figure has risen to roughly 51 openings as of November 1999.

However, critics complain that home helpers receive poor pay and little job stability. At present most home helpers are part-time workers who make between 800 and 1,100 yen per hour. In the future nursing care may even be a good part-time job for college students who seek an after-school job. Yet, a certain amount of training and a professional attitude is required in dealing with the elderly.

Full-time nursing care workers make between 160,000 and 200,000 yen a month, including various benefits. Unfortunately, this is not a very good income for the work they do. Therefore, most people who work as home helpers have a second job to supplement family income. Yet, in spite of the low pay, many find the work rewarding.

Nichii Gakkan Co. hopes to secure 24,000 home helpers nationwide in the near future, while looking into ways of improving their working conditions. To secure the services of capable home helpers, the company plans to adopt a new wage system based on a worker's experience.

The Welfare and Labor Ministry is also planning to improve the working conditions of home helpers. The Ministry will give financial assistance to corporations and non-profit organizations that provide nursing care services. Under this plan one-third to one-half of the wages of nursing care workers hired by those organizations will be subsidized for a year. It is important to improve working conditions to attract able helpers. However, companies which provide nursing care cannot predict what will happen once the nursing care insurance system starts.

Notes: job opening「求人」 critics「批評家，評論家」 per hour「1時間につき」 a certain amount of「ある一定の」 deal with「取り扱う」 supplement「補足」 one-third「3分の1」 clerk「店員」 subsidize ...「～に補助金を与える」 predict「予測する」

A 本文に合うように，文中の（　　）の中から適語を選びましょう。

1. The nursing care insurance system for the elderly went into effect in (1999 / 2000 / 2025).

2. The number of openings for home helpers now in Tokyo has become (twice / thirteen times / three times) as large as that of one year ago.

3. Nichii Gakkan Co. is going to adopt a new wage system based on (the salary / the experience / the character) of the employees.

4. Under the new plan by the Welfare and Labor Ministry (at least 30 / more than 50 / about 80) percent to one-half of nursing care wages for workers hired by non-profit organizations and corporations will be subsidized for a year.

B 本文の内容を踏まえて，下の質問に答えましょう。

1. What should be done to attract capable home helpers?

    (　　　　) (　　　　　　) should be improved.

2. What is the Welfare and Labor Ministry going to do?

    The ministry will give (　　　　　) (　　　　　　) to corporations and non-profit organizations.

3. What is difficult for nursing care services to predict?

    The companies cannot predict (　　　　　) (　　　　　) (　　　　　　) once the nursing care system starts.

WRITING PRACTICE

▶READINGの英文を参考にして，次の日本語を英語に直しましょう。

1. 介護の仕事は，放課後のアルバイトを探している大学生にとっていい仕事です。

2. ホームヘルパーには，家族を養っていけるだけの十分な給料が支払われるべきです。

3. 介護専門職には，新しい賃金体系が採用されるでしょう。

11 SERVICE DOGS STRIVE FOR OFFICIAL RECOGNITION AMID IGNORANCE

障害者を支える犬は盲導犬だけでしょうか？

障害を持つ人々に付き添い，支えるために特別に訓練された犬としては盲導犬が知られていますが，実は障害の種類に応じて訓練された犬はほかにもいるのです。こうした動物に対する私たちの理解は十分でしょうか。

WARM-UP DIALOG

CD TRACKS 21–22

▶日本語を参考に，CD を聴いて（　　　）に適切な語を入れましょう。

Setsuko: What are service dogs?
Naoko: They are dogs which help the handicapped.
Setsuko: Are they the same (1　　　) guide dogs for the blind?
Naoko: No. they are quite different. A service dog does (2　　　) than just help the blind.
Setsuko: What do you mean?
Naoko: Well, a service dog helps people to (3　　　) on their clothes or to pick up objects from the floor.
Setsuko: What (4　　　) can they do?
Naoko: Well, they can even open and close refrigerators to bring food to their owner.
Setsuko: Well, they are more (5　　　) pets. They are excellent companions.

節子：介助犬ってどんな犬なの？
尚子：障害者を手伝う犬よ。
節子：盲導犬と同じなの？
尚子：いえ，全然違う。介助犬は目の不自由な人を助けること以外に多くのことも出来るのよ。
節子：どういうこと？
尚子：そうね。飼い主が服を着たり，床にあるものを取り上げるのを手伝うの。
節子：ほかにどんなことが出来るの？
尚子：主人の食べ物を取り出すために冷蔵庫を開けたり閉めたりもできるのよ。
節子：じゃあ，ペットなんてものじゃなくって，立派な友だちですね。

FOCUS ON KEY WORDS

▶次の1から5の単語の意味を，a～eより選んで，線で結びましょう。

1. to be paralyzed　　　　　　・　　　　　・ a. バイク事故
2. motorcycle accident　　　　・　　　　　・ b. 障害に直面する
3. to limit power in one's hands ・　　　　　・ c. 麻痺する
4. a guide dog　　　　　　　・　　　　　・ d. 手の自由が利かない
5. to face obstacles　　　　　・　　　　　・ e. 盲導犬

GETTING READY TO READ

▶次の（　　）に，下の語群から適語を選んで入れてみましょう。

1. A service dog is a dog which is especially trained to help handicapped people with daily activities such as (　　　　　) and picking up objects.
   介助犬とは，障害者が服を着たり物を取り上げたりするなど，日常の活動を支援できるように特別に訓練された犬のことです。

2. Cynthia, a Labrador Retriever, is a service dog who helps her master who was paralyzed in a highway (　　　　　) thirteen years ago.
   シンシアは，ラブラドル・レトリーバ犬で，13年前に交通事故で麻痺障害になった主人を支援する介助犬です。

3. Japan Air Systems was the first (　　　　　) to allow a service dog to accompany her master on a flight from Osaka to Sapporo.
   日本エアシステムは，障害者が大阪から札幌まで搭乗する際に介助犬がその主人に同伴することを許した最初の航空会社です。

4. Service dogs for the handicapped are different from (　　　　　) dogs for the blind in that they have no legal status.
   障害者のための介助犬は，法律で資格が認められていないという点で，盲導犬とは区別されている。

> accident / patrol / dressing / to dress / guide / lead / airline / bus line

READING PASSAGE

▶英文を読んで，設問A，Bに答えましょう。

　The rights of working dogs was recognized when Japan Air Systems allowed Cynthia to accompany her disabled owner on a flight to Sapporo from Osaka. Cynthia is a dog especially trained to help the handicapped.

　The dog appeared to be completely relaxed on the flight although some people were worried that she would become nervous during takeoff and landing. The six-year old Labrador Retriever is one of just a handful of dogs in the nation trained to help disabled people with a variety of daily activities, including dressing and picking up objects. Although there are estimated to be 2,000 such registered dogs in service in the United States, Japan is far behind with only about 14.

　Cynthia's owner has been using a wheelchair since he was paralyzed in a motorcycle accident 13 years ago. He is unable to move his legs and has limited power in his arms and hands. Cynthia can understand about 50 commands, switches lights on and off for him, fetches items from the refrigerator and helps him with his shopping.

　Yoshimoto Kimura, Cynthia's owner, was traveling to Sapporo to attend a special event to raise public awareness of service dogs. Three other dogs whose owners are blind took the same flight. They were a service dog, a 'hearing' dog whose owner is deaf and a dog specially trained to help disabled and elderly people during rehabilitation.

　Unlike guide dogs who have special provisions under the Road Traffic Law, service dogs have no official or legal status. As a result they and their owners face legal problems. The use of public transportation is one of them. In general, permission must be obtained before owners can take their dogs onto most subways, trains and airplanes.

Notes：on a flight「搭乗する」　take off and landing「離着陸する」　be worried「心配している」　a handful of「少数の」　be far behind「ずいぶん遅れている」　have limited power「十分動かない」　command「命令，指令」　provision「条項，規定」　official or legal status「公的，合法的な地位」

A 本文に合うように，文中の（　）の中から適語を選びましょう。

1. The dog on the plane was completely relaxed, though officials (had expected / had been afraid / had been glad) that she would become nervous.

2. As for the estimated number of registered service dogs, Japan is (not so different from / far behind / ahead of) the United States.

3. Cynthia can understand about 50 commands (except / including / excluding) ones which help her owner with his shopping.

4. In Japan, (since / before / after) Cynthia was recognized as an authorized service dog, public awareness of service dogs has changed for the better.

B 本文の内容を踏まえて，下の質問に答えましょう。

1. What is the important role played by the service dog, Cynthia?

   Cynthia was the first working dog that was allowed to (　　　　) (　　　　) (　　　　) (　　　　) on a flight and since then, the rights of working dogs have been recognized.

2. What is the difference between a service dog and a guide dog under the Road Traffic Law in Japan?

   Guide dogs have (　　　　) or (　　　　) status under the Road Traffic Law but the service dogs do not.

3. What was the purpose of Cynthia's owner attending the special event in Sapporo?

   The purpose of his attending the event was (　　　　) (　　　　) (　　　　) (　　　　) of service dogs.

WRITING PRACTICE

▶READINGの英文を参考にして，次の日本語を英語に直しましょう。

1. 最近，電車の中で盲導犬が障害者に付き添っているのをよく見かけます。

2. 電灯をつけたり消したりすることを訓練された犬は，まだ日本では少ない。

3. 私たちは盲導犬についての意識を高める必要があります。

12 BABY-SITTER EXAM AIMS TO IMPROVE CARE

安心して子どもをベビーシッターにまかせるためには？

男女共同参画社会にあって母親が働いている家庭にとっては信頼できるベビーシッターを得ることは大きな関心事となります。そのために，どのような取り組みがなされようとしているのでしょうか。

WARM-UP DIALOG

CD TRACKS 23-24

▶日本語を参考に，CD を聴いて（　　）に適切な語を入れましょう。

Yoko: Are you (¹　　　) this weekend?
Hiromi: Yes, I'm studying (²　　　) an exam.
Yoko: Oh? But I thought the term exams were (³　　　).
Hiromi: Well, this is a different kind of exam.
Yoko: What (⁴　　　) of an exam are you taking?
Hiromi: It's an exam for becoming a baby-sitter.
Yoko: I've never heard of such a test. Why do you need an exam for such a job?
Hiromi: Well, being a baby-sitter is not easy. It requires a lot of responsibility.
Yoko: Yes, that's true. And also a (⁵　　　) of patience.
Hiromi: But, I love children so I hope I can become a good baby-sitter.

洋子：今週末，いそがしい？
裕美：試験のために勉強があるの。
洋子：そう？もう定期試験は終ったのでしょう？
裕美：試験といっても，学校の分ではないの。
洋子：何の試験を受けるの？
裕美：ベビーシッターになるための試験よ。
洋子：聞いたことないわ。その仕事にどうして試験が必要なの？
裕美：この仕事も楽にはなれないのよ。責任が伴うでしょう？
洋子：ほんとよね。それに忍耐力もいるしね。
裕美：でも，私，子どもが好きだからいいベビーシッターになれると思う。

FOCUS ON KEY WORDS

▶次の1から5の単語の意味を，a〜eより選んで，線で結びましょう。

1. baby-sitting service　　・　　　・ a. 世間の関心
2. accident prevention　　・　　　・ b. 託児業
3. infant growth　　　　　・　　　・ c. 事故防止
4. private nursery　　　　・　　　・ d. 民間託児所
5. public concern　　　　 ・　　　・ e. 幼児発育

GETTING READY TO READ

▶次の（　　）に，下の語群から適語を選んで入れてみましょう。

1. A certification will be available concerning the reliability of baby-sitters so that parents can better (　　　　) a suitable sitter for their children.
   自分の子どもにふさわしい人を選ぶためにベビーシッターの信頼性を示す証明書を利用することが出来ます。

2. Companies offering the services of sitters can specify a certain skill which the baby-sitter may possess, such (　　　　) the ability to teach English.
   ベビーシッターを派遣する会社は，その人が例えば英語を教えることが出来るといったある種の特技を持っていることを明記することができます。

3. Although the baby-sitter certification is valid only (　　　　) five years, additional training sessions may be taken to keep it valid.
   ベビーシッターの証明書は有効期間は5年ですが，更に研修を積むことで有効期間を延長することが可能です。

4. Parents who use baby-sitter services often complain that the charge is too (　　　　) and that they didn't always receive the same sitter for their children.
   ベビーシッターの派遣制度を利用する親は，費用が高すぎるとか，同じ人を継続して来てもらうことができないなど，不満をもっています。

   as / so / choose / take / for / by / high / much

READING PASSAGE

▶英文を読んで，設問Ⓐ，Ⓑに答えましょう。

The Tokyo based All-Japan Baby-Sitter Association will introduce an optional certificate for employees of professional baby-sitting services. The purpose is to improve the standard of private care for infants.

The certificate addresses the public concern about the reliability of baby-sitting services. This certification will help families to find trustworthy baby-sitters for their children.

Recently, there has been a demand for such services as baby-sitting becomes more popular. Companies offer the services of baby-sitters and advertise their special skills such as an ability to teach English to infants. Yet, parents are sometimes worried about leaving their children in the hands of strangers no matter how qualified they are.

The proposed examination is to cover knowledge of infant growth, health-care and accident prevention for young children. People who wish to take the examination will be required first to complete introductory baby-sitter training classes before the test. Those who pass the test will be presented with a certificate valid for five years.

The average charge of a baby-sitter is 1,500 yen an hour. Working mothers are the biggest users of such services. However, about half of them complained that the charge of the service was too high. Others said there was not enough information when trying to select a company. Another common complaint was that they did not always receive the same baby-sitter for their children. Some parents still did not have enough confidence in baby-sitting services.

However, some parents think that baby-sitting is only a part-time job for students. This idea needs to be changed. Baby-sitters are responsible for the lives of children, so an exam system to guarantee the quality of baby-sitters needs to begin as soon as possible.

Notes： certificate「証明書」 reliability「信頼性」 trustworthy「信用できる」 no matter how...「いかに～であろうとも」 qualified「資格のある」 valid「有効な」 complain「愚痴をこぼす」 confidence「確信」 be responsible for ...「～に責任を負う」

A 本文に合うように，文中の（　　）の中から適語を選びましょう。

1. The purpose of introducing optional certificates is to improve the standard of (infants / professional baby-sitters / parents).

2. Those who receive the certificate will be qualified to work as baby-sitters for (at least five years / more than five years / less than five years).

3. The demand for such reliable baby-sitting services will (increase / decrease / change) in the future.

4. One of the complaints of mothers who use baby-sitting services is that they have (little / too much / good) information about selecting a reliable company.

B 本文の内容を踏まえて，下の質問に答えましょう。

1. Why will the All-Japan Baby-Sitter Association introduce the optional certificate?

   Because it is necessary to (　　　　) the (　　　　) of private care of (　　　　).

2. What worry do parents have regarding baby-sitting services?

   They worry about leaving (　　　　) (　　　　) in the hands of (　　　　).

3. What are the common complaints of the mothers concerning baby-sitting services?

   Mothers commonly complain that the charge is (　　　　) (　　　　) and that they did not always receive (　　　　) (　　　　) (　　　　) - (　　　　).

(WRITING PRACTICE)

▶READINGの英文を参考にして，次の日本語を英語に直しましょう。

1. 日本にはまだベビーシッターは普及していませんが，今後は需要が増すでしょう。

2. ベビーシッターが利用できても，親が他人の手に子供を安心して任せるようになるには，若干時間がかかるでしょう。

3. 働いている母親は，子どものために信頼できるベビーシッターを見つけることに苦労します。

13. JAPAN BRACES FOR LIFE AS OLDEST NATION

世界一の長寿国日本，高齢者の世話は誰がするのでしょうか？

人類が未だ経験したことがない速さで高齢化が進み，長寿国となる日本は世界に先駆けて高齢者介護の問題に対処しなければなりません。生涯を社会や家族のために尽くした高齢者の介護は，誰が受け持つのでしょう？

WARM-UP DIALOG

CD TRACKS 25–26

▶日本語を参考に，CD を聴いて（　　　）に適切な語を入れましょう。

Yukako: Today we are having a (1　　　) party for my grandmother.
Takako: Oh, that's great! How old will she be?
Yukako: It's very special. She'll be one hundred.
Takako: It (2　　　) be wonderful to have lived so long.
Yukako: But, today it is not (3　　　) for someone to live to be a hundred.
Takako: I (4　　　) you're right. My grandfather will be ninety-five next month.
Yukako: Would you like to live to be a hundred?
Takako: I don't know. I'm (5　　　) there will be no one to care for me.
Yukako: That's why it is important for us to stay healthy.
Takako: Yes, so that when we get old we can enjoy life.

由香子：今日はおばあちゃんの誕生日をお祝いするのよ。
多賀子：そう。いいわね。おいくつになるの？
由香子：驚くわよ。100歳よ。
多賀子：そんなに長生きできるってすばらしいことね。
由香子：でも，今日では100歳まで生きても珍しくないわよ。
多賀子：その通りかもね。私の祖父も来月で95歳だもの。
由香子：あなたも100歳まで生きたい？
多賀子：わからない。誰も面倒を見てくれる人がいないのじゃないかな？
由香子：そのとおり，だから健康でなくてはならないのよ。
多賀子：そう。年を取っても人生を楽しむことができないとね。

FOCUS ON KEY WORDS

▶次の１から５の単語の意味を，ａ〜ｅより選んで，線で結びましょう。

1. pension system　　・　　　　・ a. 低出生率
2. the low birthrate　・　　　　・ b. 介護者
3. old population　　・　　　　・ c. 高齢者人口
4. elder-care business ・　　　　・ d. 高齢者介護事業
5. caregiver　　　　　・　　　　・ e. 年金制度

GETTING READY TO READ

▶次の（　　　）に，下の語群から適語を選んで入れてみましょう。

1. The Japanese will soon have the world's oldest (　　　　) as their country ages faster than any other country in the world.
   日本は世界で最も速く高齢化が進んでいるので，やがて世界一の高齢者国になるでしょう。

2. Japan's aging society has put a great responsibility and obligation (　　　　) the younger generation to take care of their aging parents.
   高齢化が進む日本では，親の介護を担う若い世代に大きな責任と負担を負わすことになるでしょう。

3. Although many elderly people have enough money saved to support themselves for the (　　　　) of their lives, they still worry about getting old.
   多くのお年寄りは，自らの余生で誰にも迷惑をかけまいと十分な預金をしていますが，それでも年を取ることに不安をもっています。

4. Many older people see the younger (　　　　) as selfish without the same sense of responsibility as past generations.
   多くの高齢者は，今日の若者は自己中心的で自分たちが持っているような貢献しようという感覚は持ち合わせていないと思っています。

generation / age / rest / spare / to / on / time / population

READING PASSAGE

▶英文を読んで，設問Ⓐ，Ⓑに答えましょう。

　Japan's society is aging faster than any other country in the world. It has the world's longest life span and one of the lowest birthrates. Japan is expected to displace Sweden by 2005 as having the planet's oldest population.

　This is already straining pension and health care systems, and Japan's economy will soon have to care for more elderly people with fewer workers. In the early 21st century Japan's elderly society will be something no other country has ever experienced.

　Benesse Corporation originally specialized in education, but now is going into the elderly-care business. The company has graduated 2,500 people in a 'home-helper' training course and yearly the number increases. The company also runs a home helper service for people caring for elderly relatives at home.

　The government hopes to encourage other companies to follow Bennese's example. The government hopes to shift the cost of financing back to the consumer. Many of the elderly have saved enough money to care for themselves and have assets to live on for the rest of their lives.

　Japan has few nursing homes compared to other developed countries and most people assume their children will care for them when they get old. At present, more than half of the elderly live with their children or other relatives.

　Some people feel, however, that it is unrealistic to expect families to take care of their elder members. At the center of this debate are Japan's primary caregivers: women. Housewives are expected to raise children by themselves and later to spend their middle-age taking care of their husbands' parents. Some women, however, want their own careers and resent being caretakers for the elderly members of their family. Moreover, many do not expect their children to care for them when they get old. They see their children as independent without the traditional sense of obligation.

　To solve this issue of an aging society, we should take these women's concerns into consideration and also take advantage of the improved nursing care insurance system as proposed by the government.

Notes: displace …「〜に取って代わる」 specialize in …「〜を専業とする」 asset「資産」
compared to …「〜と比較すると」 assume …「〜と思う，信ずる」 resent「不快に思う」
sense of obligation「義務感」 take advantage of …「〜を活用する」

A 本文に合うように，文中の（　　）の中から適語を選びましょう。

1. The government expects companies to get into the elder-care business by shifting the cost of care to (themselves / the governments / the elderly).

2. There are (more / less / the same) nursing homes in Japan than in other developed countries.

3. Japanese housewives generally spend their (early / middle / old) years taking care of their children and later, when they are middle-aged, they care for their husband's parents.

4. (More / Many / Only a few) of today's parents think it is their children's responsibility to take care of them when they become old.

B 本文の内容を踏まえて，下の質問に答えましょう。

1. Give two reasons why Japanese society is rapidly aging.
   One reason is it has the world's (　　　)(　　　)(　　　) and the other is it has one of the (　　　)(　　　).

2. What does Benesse Corporation specialize in?
   It specializes in (　　　) and the (　　　) business.

3. Why are the government's plans to expect families to take care of their elder members unrealistic?
   Because some women want (　　　)(　　　)(　　　) and many don't want to be (　　　) for (　　　)(　　　)(　　　) when they get old.

WRITING PRACTICE

▶READINGの英文を参考にして，次の日本語を英語に直しましょう。

1. 日本は急速に高齢化が進行しており，年金についての関心が高まっています。

2. 日本は，世界で出生率が最も低い国の一つであり，これがわが国の高齢化を早めています。

3. 今日では，年を取っても子どもに面倒を見てもらうことを望まない人が増えています。

14. EX-NISSAN CHIEF SAYS NATION IS ILL-PREPARED FOR AN AGING SOCIETY

どうして日本は，高齢化社会への対応に遅れてしまったのでしょうか？

日本を物質的に豊にした高度成長は，一方ですべてをお金で換算する価値観を培い，道徳的頽廃をもたらし，やがて来る高齢化社会への対応を見落としたとする，日産の久米元社長の意見をもとに考えてみましょう。

WARM-UP DIALOG

CD TRACKS 27–28

▶ 日本語を参考に，CD を聴いて（　　　）に適切な語を入れましょう。

Etsuko: I sometimes worry about getting old.
Satoshi: Well, everybody does.
Etsuko: Yes, but I (1　　　) who will look after me.
Satoshi: Don't be silly. You'll always have your family to care for you.
Etsuko: Well, I'm not (2　　　) about that. After all, my children will have their own children to take care of.
Satoshi: I'm sure they will take care of you, too!
Etsuko: I don't know. The young people today do not have the same (3　　　) of responsibility as past generations did.
Satoshi: But today's society is changing.
Etsuko: Do you think so?
Satoshi: Yes, the young people today are very much (4　　　) of the problems of an aging society.
Etsuko: It's true, but they are more (5　　　) from their parents, too.

悦子：私は時々年を取ったあとのことを考えて不安になるの。
智史：うん，皆そうだよ。
悦子：そのとおり。だけど，私は世話をしてくれる人がいそうにないの。
智史：馬鹿なこと言っちゃいけないよ。いつも家族がいるじゃない。
悦子：そりゃ疑問よ。だって私の子供たちも，ゆくゆく子供ができてその面倒を見なければならないもの。
智史：あなたの面倒も見てくれますよ。
悦子：それはどうかしら。今時の若い人は古い世代が持つ責任感なんてもっていないわよ。
智史：でも時代は変わりつつあるよ。
悦子：そう思う？
智史：今日の若者は，高齢化が進む社会の課題は分かっているよ。
悦子：そう。同時に，自分は自分，親のことは知らないという感覚もね。

FOCUS ON KEY WORDS

▶次の1から5の単語の意味を，a～eより選んで，線で結びましょう。

1. nursing facility　　・　　・a. 入院している
2. to be hospitalized　　・　　・b. 道徳的頽廃
3. moral decay　　・　　・c. 介護施設
4. to sacrifice one's life　・　　・d. 消費社会
5. consumer society　　・　　・e. 自分の生活を犠牲にする

GETTING READY TO READ

▶次の（　　）に，下の語群から適語を選んで入れてみましょう。

1. Mr. Kume confessed that taking care of his elderly mother was a period of (　　　　) and personal stress for himself and his family.
   久米氏は，自分の年老いた母の介護をした時期は，家族にとっても自分にとっても経済的にも一人の人間としてもストレスのある時期であったと告白しました。

2. Economic (　　　　) has created a society more interested in consumerism than the problem of taking care of the elderly.
   経済成長は，高齢者の介護の問題よりも消費主義に興味を持つ社会にしてしまいました。

3. This is now a time of (　　　　) decay and people have failed to build a loving society where the wealth is equally shared.
   今日は，道徳的頽廃の時期であり，富を等しく分け合う愛のある社会にはなっていません。

4. Both business and the public are (　　　　) for the current neglect to respond to the needs of an aging society.
   今日の高齢化社会のニーズに応えられないことについては，実業界も国民大衆も双方に責任があります。

---

growth / length / physical / financial / duty / responsible / mental / moral

READING PASSAGE

▶英文を読んで，設問Ⓐ，Ⓑに答えましょう。

　Japan is far behind other developed countries in creating a caring system for the elderly. There has been much criticism about this neglect.

　Yutaka Kume is a former president of Nissan Motor Co. whose mother-in-law had been living with the family for fifteen years. During this time she was hospitalized when she fell and broke her leg. In the three years before her death at the age of 93 she was bedridden at the Kume's home. For Mr. Kume this was a period of considerable stress for his family both financially and personally. Yet, it did not interfere with his job.

　Nevertheless, Japan is not prepared emotionally for its aging society. Mr. Kume is only one of many Japanese who face the same problems. Japanese managers and salarimen who worked long hours to become successful are not necessarily the cause of the problem. Yet, perhaps Japan achieved economic development too fast. People did not pay attention to their daily lives and society lost a great deal.

　It can be said that the country's postwar economic excellence is mainly responsible for this deficiency. Japan's dramatic economic growth in the 1960s was a matter of both pride and regret. It was the postwar generation that made the miracle possible.

　Economic growth created a consumer society which has not helped the growth of a caring society. Many feel today that everything is measured in money. This has created a moral decay and a failure for Japan to become a loving society where the wealth of the many is shared by every individual.

　Both the business sector and the public are responsible for this widespread neglect and, unfortunately, they fail to respond to the immediate problem. The increase in the aging population will create many different challenges which the government cannot solve by itself. Therefore, corporations and individuals must become more independent and find better solutions to the problems of everyday life.

Notes： bedridden「寝たきりの」　confess「白状する」　deficiency「欠陥」　a great deal「たくさん，相当に」　business sector「実業界」　be responsible for ...「〜に責任を負う」　be shared「共有する，分けあう」　corporation「会社」

A 本文に合うように、文中の（　　）の中から適語を選びましょう。

1. To Mr. Kume there was a period of considerable stress in caring for his mother-in-law but this had (nothing / much / something) to do with his job.

2. Managers of big companies often can't (live / spend / waste) much time on their private lives.

3. In a consumer society, people are apt to think (too little / too much / nothing) of money.

4. A loving society means a society where there is (not so great / no / so great) difference in wealth among its people.

B 本文の内容を踏まえて、下の質問に答えましょう。

1. Why is Japan responsible for not preparing for its aging society?

   Because Japan's economic growth (　　　　) (　　　　) (　　　　).

2. What aspect of Japanese thinking has created a moral decay in Japan?

   Many Japanese feel today that everything is (　　　　) (　　　　) (　　　　).

3. What is necessary to solve the problems of everyday life in an aging society?

   Corporations and individuals must (　　　　) (　　　　) (　　　　) in order to solve the problems of everyday life.

WRITING PRACTICE

▶READINGの英文を参考にして、次の日本語を英語に直しましょう。

1. 私の祖母は3年間家で寝たきりの生活となり、その間家族みんなで介護にあたりました。

2. 戦後の経済成長は生活状態を良くしましたが、一方ですべてを金で計るというモラルの腐敗をもたらしました。

3. 高齢化社会では、政府だけでは片付かない様々な問題が起こってきます。

15 SIMULATED PATIENT ENABLES RISK-FREE MEDICAL TRAINING

マネキンが医療や介護教育の手助けになるでしょうか？

人間の種々の機能に反応するソフトを内蔵したダミーを医学や看護の訓練の場で用いることで，人間にありがちな誤りを防ごうという取り組みの話です。医療器具や薬品の発達と人間のミス，事故防止について考えましょう。

WARM-UP DIALOG

CD TRACKS 29–30

▶日本語を参考に，CD を聴いて（　　）に適切な語を入れましょう。

Takako: I hear you are studying to be a nurse, Natsuko. Is that true?
Natsuko: Yes, I hope someday to work (1　　　　) a hospital.
Takako: Your studies must be very difficult.
Natsuko: Yes, we must know a lot about chemistry and medicine.
Takako: It requires a great responsibility to care for those (2　　　　) are very ill.
Natsuko: Yes, it does. Sometimes when we treat (3　　　　) they may have a very bad reaction to the drugs we give.
Takako: You must become very (4　　　　) when this happens.
Natsuko: Not really. Because our patients aren't really (5　　　　).
Takako: You mean your patients aren't human?!
Natsuko: Yes, they are computerized dummies. They are only mannequins.

孝子：あなたは，看護婦になるための勉強をしているのね？
夏子：ええ，将来は病院で働きたいの。
孝子：勉強は大変でしょう。
夏子：ええ。化学や医学のことをずいぶん学ばなければならないのよ。
孝子：そりゃ，重い病気の人の看護は責任が大きいでしょうからね。
夏子：そうよ。薬を投与して患者さんに悪い症状が出たりするとね。
孝子：そんなことが起きると心配でしょうにね。
夏子：そうでもないの。患者さんは，生きた人間でないから。
孝子：人間でないって？
夏子：そう，コンピュータで制御されたダミーなの。マネキンが反応するの。

FOCUS ON KEY WORDS

▶次の1から5の単語の意味を、a～eより選んで、線で結びましょう。

1. simulator　　　・　　　　・a. 患者
2. patient　　　　・　　　　・b. 等身大の訓練用人形
3. life-sized dummy ・　　　　・c. 注射する
4. medical profession ・　　　・d. 医業
5. inject　　　　 ・　　　　・e. 模擬装置

GETTING READY TO READ

▶次の（　　）に、下の語群から適語を選んで入れてみましょう。

1. The dummy is so connected that monitors can immediately detect a problem just as (　　　　) it were human.
   モニターに接続されているダミーは、あたかも生身の人間であるかのようにすぐに悪いところを見つけることが出来ます。

2. Simulated dummies are much in demand both in the military and medical schools to (　　　　) young professionals in their work.
   模擬装置を内蔵するダミーは、若い専門職の人々が仕事に必要な訓練を積むために軍隊でも医学の学校でも需要が多い。

3. A health (　　　　) can be triggered in the dummy which requires the medical student to make quick decisions in an emergency.
   病状が危険な状態に陥るとダミーが反応し、学生は危機状態の中でなさねばならない迅速な医学的判断を下すことが求められます。

4. The technology of simulated dummies is especially useful in the treatment of little children who react to (　　　　) quite differently than adults.
   この模擬装置を内蔵するダミーの技術は、医薬品に大人とは全く異なった反応を示す小さい子どもの処置の際に特に役立ちます。

> though / when / train / help / crisis / drugs / mistake / operation

READING PASSAGE

▶英文を読んで、設問A, Bに答えましょう。

　The breathing tube missed and the doctors were afraid that the patient would die but it was only a little frightening. Why? Because the patient was only a dummy named Stan. Stan is short for Standard Man and is a dummy used in the training of nurses. The dummy is connected to monitors that immediately display a problem just as though the dummy were really human. This allows doctors and nurses to get practice without endangering the life of a live patient.

　These human dummies called simulators are part of a comprehensive training program for the medical professions. They are used in nursing schools, community colleges and other health science programs. They are much in demand in medical schools and the military. Furthermore, these simulated dummies are also useful for training in response to weapons of mass destruction, chemical or biological disasters.

　These human simulators, however, are quite expensive and cost around 18 million yen each for a top-of-the-line model. They come with precise physical characteristics of the human body. They are also programmed with software allowing the creation of thousands of real-life emergency situations. The software is run by a computer which makes the life-sized dummy react like a human being. The mannequin can also duplicate the exact characteristics of an individual patient.

　Someone running the simulator can choose a program which can trigger a health crisis requiring the student to make quick decisions to respond to the emergency. The dummy can also react to as many as 70 different drugs which are injected from bar-coded syringes that the computer can identify.

　This new technology is especially useful in the treatment of children since many doctors get little hands-on training in the treatment of young patients. The young are not merely small adults. Physically they are quite different from grown-ups and react quite differently to drugs and types of treatment. Although this technology of using dummies is primarily for the training of nurses, it can also be used for those who are studying social welfare.

Notes: simulator「模擬装置」 comprehensive「総合的な」 to be in demand「需要がある」 top-of-the-line「最高の地位の」 duplicate「複製する，2倍にする」 trigger「(反応などを) 引き起こす」 syringe「注射器」

A 本文に合うように，文中の（　　）の中から適語を選びましょう。

1. When the breathing tube missed, the doctors were (just a little frightened / very afraid / frightened very much) because the patient was only a dummy.

2. The simulated dummy responds as precisely as if it were (a real person / a living animal / a monitor).

3. The top-of-the-line model costs (as much as / less than / more than) 18 million yen.

4. Besides being used in medicine, the simulated dummy can also be used for the training in response to (airplane crashes / chemical disasters / household accidents).

B 本文の内容を踏まえて，下の質問に答えましょう。

1. Why didn't the doctors fear for the life of the patient when the breathing tube was missed?

   Because the patient was (　　　　) (　　　　) (　　　　).

2. Where are the human simulators used?

   They are used in (　　　　) (　　　　), (　　　　) (　　　　) and (　　　　) (　　　　) (　　　　) (　　　　).

3. Why is simulator technology especially useful in the treatment of children?

   Because children are physically quite (　　　　) (　　　　) (　　　　)-(　　　　) and (　　　　) (　　　　) (　　　　) to drugs.

WRITING PRACTICE

▶READINGの英文を参考にして，次の日本語を英語に直しましょう。

1. この車は一定の制限スピード内で走るようにソフトが組み込まれています。

2. 新しい技術が，子供の患者の治療に大いに役立ちます。

3. その人形は，薬に素早く反応するソフトが組み込まれています。

本書にはカセットテープ(別売)があります

English for Social Welfare
―福祉の英語―

2002年 1 月20日　初版発行
2021年 9 月30日　重版発行

著　者　William M. Balsamo
　　　　阿　部　敏　之
発行者　福　岡　正　人
発行所　株式会社　金星堂
(〒101-0051) 東京都千代田区神田神保町 3-21
Tel. 営業部 (03)3263-3828　編集部 (03)3263-3997　Fax. (03)3263-0716
E-mail: 営業部 text@kinsei-do.co.jp

印刷所／加藤文明社　製本所／松島製本　1-11-3753
落丁・乱丁本はお取り替えいたします

ISBN978-4-7647-3753-2 C1082